WHAT IS ELECTRICAL ENERGY?

JOE GREEK

Britannica®
Educational Publishing

IN ASSOCIATION WITH

ROSEN
EDUCATIONAL SERVICES

Published in 2018 by Britannica Educational Publishing (a trademark of Encyclopædia Britannica, Inc.) in association with The Rosen Publishing Group, Inc.
29 East 21st Street, New York, NY 10010

Distributed exclusively by Rosen Publishing.
To see additional Britannica Educational Publishing titles, go to rosenpublishing.com.

First Edition

Britannica Educational Publishing
J.E. Luebering: Executive Director, Core Editorial
Mary Rose McCudden: Editor, Britannica Student Encyclopedia

Rosen Publishing
Amelie von Zumbusch: Editor
Nelson Sá: Art Director
Nicole Russo-Duca: Designer
Cindy Reiman: Photography Manager
Sherri Jackson: Photo Researcher

Library of Congress Cataloging-in-Publication Data

Names: Greek, Joe, author.
Title: What is electrical energy? / Joe Greek.
Description: First edition. | New York, NY : Britannica Educational Publishing in association with Rosen Educational Services, 2018. | Series: Let's find out! Forms of energy | Audience: 1-4.
Identifiers: LCCN 2016056466 | ISBN 9781680486995 (library bound book ; alk. paper) | ISBN 9781680486971 (pbk. book ; alk. paper) | ISBN 9781680486988 (6 pack ; alk. paper)
Subjects: LCSH: Electricity—Juvenile literature. | Electric power—Juvenile literature.
Classification: LCC QC527.2 .G74 2018 | DDC 537—dc23
LC record available at https://lccn.loc.gov/2016056466

Manufactured in the United States of America

CONTENTS

What Is Electrical Energy?

Energy is another word for power. Without energy, machines would not be able to work. Plants and animals would not be able to live and grow.

There are many different forms of energy. Heat and light are examples of energy you can find in the world.

Another form of energy that most people are familiar with is electrical energy, or electricity. It is very important to people. Without electrical energy, we would not have many

Energy is required for all sorts of things. For example, our bodies need energy to run.

4

People often use devices that are powered by electrical energy in their daily lives.

conveniences. From lightbulbs to televisions, electrical energy powers all sorts of things.

Electricity can be formed using machines, but it is also found in nature. A bolt of lightning is electrical energy that is suddenly released in the atmosphere.

THINK ABOUT IT

Before lightbulbs were invented, people used fire to see in the dark. What forms of energy are released from fire?

Electrical Energy at Its Core

Electrical energy is associated with the tiny building blocks of matter called atoms. Everything in the universe is made up of atoms.

At the center of an atom is a nucleus. The nucleus consists of particles called protons and neutrons. Protons carry a positive electrical charge and neutrons carry no electrical charge.

Surrounding the nucleus is a cloud of particles called electrons. Electrons carry a negative electrical charge.

All things that take up space are made up of tiny particles called atoms.

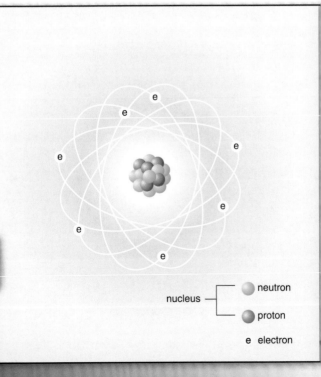

e

nucleus — ◯ neutron

● proton

e electron

Power lines are used to move electricity from one place to another over great distances.

They constantly travel in circular paths around the nucleus. Sometimes electrons from one atom will move to another atom. The moving electrons are electricity. Scientists now understand how to cause electrons to move and how to control where electrons travel. Today electricity can be formed and then delivered across small and great distances.

COMPARE AND CONTRAST

What do protons have in common with electrons and neutrons? In what ways are they different?

Negative and Positive Forces

Negative and positive charges attract each other. However, two positive charges, or two negative charges, **repel** each other. Electricity results when electrons (which have negative charges) are pushed and pulled from atom to atom.

The push and pull of negative and positive charges causes magnetism. Magnetism is a basic force of nature, like electricity and gravity. Spinning electrons form tiny magnetic forces.

VOCABULARY

To **repel** means to push away.

Magnets strongly attract objects that contain iron, steel, nickel, or cobalt.

8

An electromagnet is metal that becomes magnetic when electrons move through or near it.

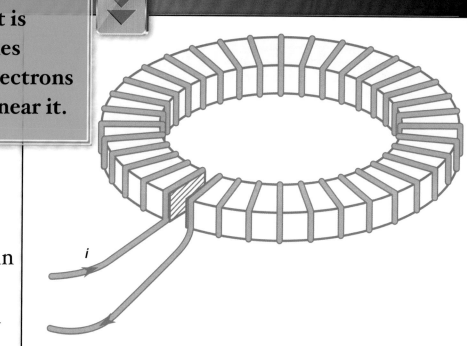

Sometimes many of the electrons in an object spin in the same direction. In these cases, all the tiny magnetic forces from the electrons add up to make the object one big magnet. Magnets have many uses. They hold papers on refrigerator doors. They are also used in credit cards, stereo speakers, and compasses.

Electricity can create magnets. As electrons move through a piece of wire they have the same effect as electrons spinning around the nucleus of an atom. This creates an electromagnet.

Conductors and Insulators

Materials that allow electricity to pass through them easily are called electrical conductors. Many metals, such as iron, steel, copper, and aluminum, are conductors. Equipment that is used to conduct electricity is often made up of metal parts.

Electric circuits are paths for moving electricity. In a simple circuit, copper wire conducts electricity from the energy source (such as a battery) to an electrical device (such as a lamp, motor, or bell).

This electrical circuit consists of a battery, a lightbulb, and a switch, connected by wires.

earphones

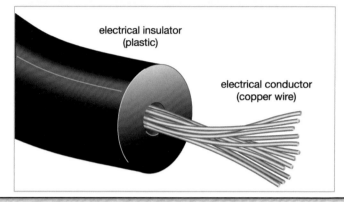

electrical insulator
(plastic)

electrical conductor
(copper wire)

Electrical wires have metal threads (conductors) with a protective covering (an insulator).

Materials that do not conduct electricity are called electrical insulators. Examples of insulators include plastic, rubber, wood, and glass. Air is also an insulator.

Most electrical objects are made using insulators to keep them safe. Plugs, for example, have plastic cases. Electrical wires are wrapped in plastic, which is flexible as well as insulating.

Think About It

Without insulators, many common devices people use would be dangerous to touch. Can you name three electrical devices you touch every day?

STATIC ELECTRICITY

Most objects have an equal amount of positive and negative charges, so they are considered neutral. They do not push or pull on each other at all electrically. However, sometimes electrons can build up in an object. Two such objects can push or pull on each other because they are no longer neutral. This push or pull from extra electrons is called static electricity.

Van de Graaff generators produce enough static electricity to make your hair stand on end!

Rubbing a balloon against one's hair can produce small amounts of static electricity.

Static electricity can cause interesting effects, like sparks or lightning bolts, when it is released. Sometimes the extra electrons build up by rubbing one object against another. For example, when one rubs a balloon against one's hair, electrons move from the balloon to the hair. Because the hairs then all have extra electrons, which all have the same kind of charge, they try to fly away from each other and end up sticking into the air like spikes.

THINK ABOUT IT

Static electricity pulls objects together or pushes them apart. What other force acts in a similar way?

ELECTRICAL ENERGY IN NATURE

Lightning is a natural form of electricity. Water droplets and ice particles inside a cloud carry electrical charges. Some charges are positive and others are negative. Lightning occurs usually when too many negative charges build up in a cloud. To balance out these negative charges, positive charges form under the cloud on the ground. Because opposite charges attract, the negative charges in the cloud want to join the positive charges below.

It's difficult for the charges to unite because air is an insulator. As the cloud grows, however, so does

egative and
sitive charges
tract to create
htning.

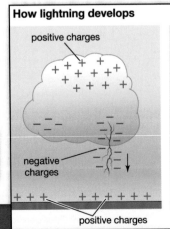

How lightning develops

positive charges

negative charges

positive charges

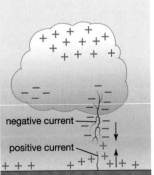

negative current

positive current

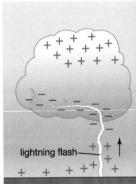

lightning flash

The sudden meeting of negative and positive charges in the air can create lightning bolts

the strength of the charges. Eventually the charges overpower the air and the cloud releases a strong, negatively charged electrical **current**.

As the negative current heads toward the ground, a positively charged current jumps from the ground to meet it. When the currents join, a bright flash is created that heads back up toward the cloud. This is a lightning flash.

VOCABULARY

An electrical **current** is a stream of moving electrons.

Electrical Energy in You

Without electrical energy and electricity, you would not be able to read this book. Every action you take is made possible by electrical signals that travel through your body.

Like everything around us, our bodies are made up of atoms. And in those atoms, there are protons, neutrons, and electrons. When the charges of these particles are out of balance, electrons move to other atoms to create balance. Electricity travels along nerve cells

Even drinking water requires the use of electrical energy.

throughout the body. Electrical signals from your brain tell your body what to do. When you turn the page of a book, your brain is sending electrical signals to your hands. Your eyes send electrical signals back to the brain about what you are reading. Unlike a lightning bolt, the electricity in your body is not dangerous.

Electrical signals are sent to and from the brain along nerve cells to control the body.

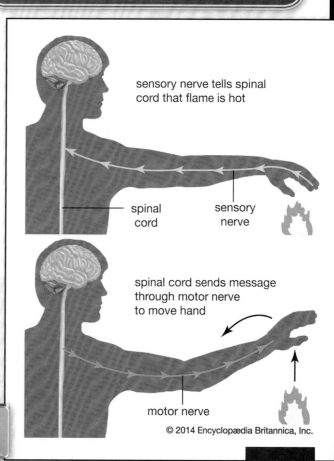

sensory nerve tells spinal cord that flame is hot

spinal cord

sensory nerve

spinal cord sends message through motor nerve to move hand

motor nerve

© 2014 Encyclopædia Britannica, Inc.

Electrical Energy Powers the World

Our world runs on electrical energy. We light our homes and schools with lamps that are powered by electricity. The cars and buses we ride in are made up of parts that require electricity.

Learning how to **generate** and deliver electricity has changed the way we live. For example, before the invention of the phone, people

Vocabulary

To **generate** something is to cause it to exist.

Electric current from a car's battery is needed to start a car.

This X-ray image shows a pacemaker in a person's chest. Many people rely on these devices.

had to write letters to communicate over long distances. Now we can call family and loved ones at anytime from anywhere in the world. Like cars, phones use electricity to work.

Electricity is also used to save lives. For example, a pacemaker is a device that sends electric signals to a person's heart. The electric signals keep the heart beating regularly if the body cannot do that on its own. Many inventions that have made survival and life easier would not exist without electricity.

Battery Power

Batteries give electric power to flashlights, radios, cell phones, handheld games, and many other types of equipment. A battery is a sort of container that stores energy until it is needed. Chemicals inside the battery store the energy. When the battery is used, the chemical energy changes into electrical energy.

Inside a battery there are two pieces of metal in a liquid or a paste. The metal parts are

◀◀ Chemical energy becomes electrical energy, and then light energy, in a flashlight.

called electrodes. The liquid or paste, called an electrolyte, is a mix of chemicals. Each electrode has a point, called a terminal, that sticks out of the battery.

THINK ABOUT IT

Batteries produce different amounts of energy. Why would a car need a larger battery than a flashlight?

When you turn a flashlight on, an outside wire links the terminals in the battery. Then the chemicals in the electrolyte cause electrons to flow from one electrode to the other. The electric current flowing through the wire makes the flashlight work.

An ordinary flashlight batter contains a mix c chemicals callec an electrolyte.

electric current

positive (+) terminal

electrode 1

electrolyte

electrode 2

insulated tube

negative (–) terminal

GENERATING AND DELIVERING ELECTRICITY

Electricity powers all sorts of devices and things we use every day. With special machines and **technology**, we are able to produce electricity and use it safely.

VOCABULARY

Technology is the use of knowledge to invent new devices or tools.

The electricity we use in our homes is generated by power plants far away.

Utility poles support power lines that deliver electricity far and wide.

A city's power plant uses machines called generators to produce a powerful electric current. Power plants need a source of energy to turn the generators that produce electricity. The moving energy of water or wind is often used to run the generators.

Generators cause a current to flow by moving a magnet past a coil of wire, which pushes electrons through the wires of the coil. The current travels through wires to houses and other buildings. More wires connect to the power outlets in rooms. When a person plugs in an iron or another electric device, the current travels into the device. The current then makes the device work.

ENERGY SOURCES FOR GENERATORS

The major source of fuel throughout the world is coal. Coal is a black or brown rock. When a power plant burns coal, it creates heat. The heat then boils water. Steam from the boiling water rotates turbines that power generators.

Thermoelectric generators boil water to generate electricity.

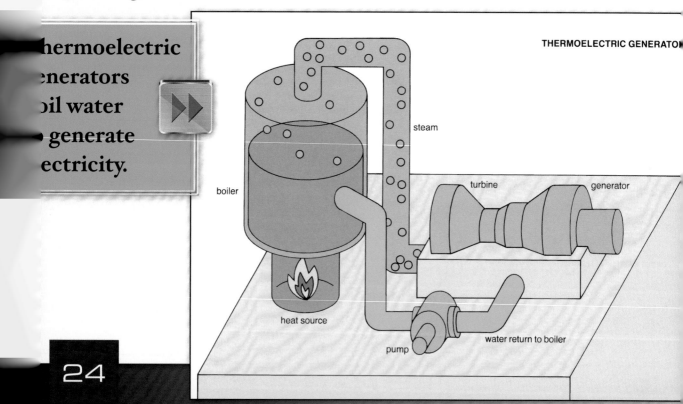

THERMOELECTRIC GENERATOR

boiler

steam

turbine

generator

heat source

pump

water return to boiler

Hydropower, or waterpower, is another energy source used to power generators. Hydroelectric power plants are usually located in dams that are built across rivers. In a dam, water is collected at a high level and is then led downward through large pipes to a lower level. The falling water rotates turbines that power generators.

Other energy sources may also be used to power generators. Coal and other fossil fuels release harmful gases when burned and can be used up. Alternative energy sources, such as water and solar power, cannot be used up and do not harm the environment.

THINK ABOUT IT

Windmills can turn moving energy into electricity. What are some benefits of using wind as an energy source?

Hydroelectric plants use moving water to produce electricity.

Measuring Electricity

Measuring electricity is important for many reasons. For one, it lets power companies know how much electrical energy a customer uses. Homes and businesses pay their power company for the amount they use. Power companies use electrical meters located outside a home or business to measure the amount of energy that has been used there. Secondly, the measurement of electricity is important for safety reasons. Different devices and products can handle only certain amounts

Electric meters show the amount of electricity being used in a location.

> **The Scottish inventor James Watt made great improvements to the steam engine.**

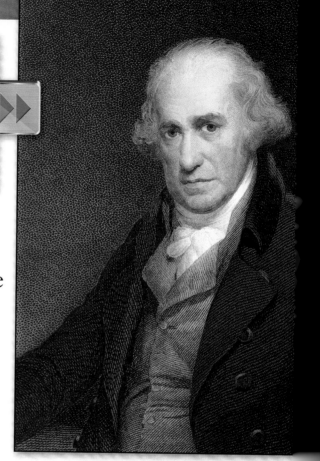

of electricity. Too much electricity can overheat or cause devices to catch on fire or explode.

Electricity is measured in units called watts. The watt is named after the inventor James Watt. A watt is a low amount of power. Small devices, such as lightbulbs, use few watts. Larger appliances and machines require more power. Electricity that larger appliances use is measured in kilowatt units.

> **VOCABULARY**
>
> A **kilowatt** is equal to one thousand watts.

Pioneers of Electrical Energy and Electricity

The ancient Greeks were the first to study electric forces. Thales was a Greek philosopher who lived about 2,500 years ago. He discovered static electricity by rubbing silk against a stone called amber. The buildup of electrons caused by the rubbing attracted feathers and bits of straw to the amber.

In the American colonies during the 1700s, Benjamin Franklin studied electricity. His experiments led to the invention of the lightning rod. That metal rod is used to protect buildings from lightning.

In 1878, the American inventor

Franklin's great curiosity led him to experiment with lightning.

Thomas Edison introduced the world to the lightbulb. For centuries, people relied on fire and eventually gas lamps to light up their homes. These could be very dangerous. Homes could catch fire and be destroyed quickly. The lightbulb and our ability to control electrical energy may have saved millions of lives to this day.

COMPARE AND CONTRAST

In what ways are lightbulbs and lightning rods similar? How are the two inventions different?

GLOSSARY

appliance A household device or piece of office equipment that runs on gas or electricity.

atmosphere The air that surrounds a planet.

atom The smallest particle of an element that has the properties of the element and can exist either alone or in combination.

chemical A substance that is formed when two or more other substances act upon one another or that is used to produce a change in another substance.

device A piece of equipment used to serve a special purpose.

electron A very small elementary particle within an atom that has a negative electric charge and travels around the nucleus of an atom.

environment All the physical surroundings on Earth, including everything living and nonliving.

fossil fuel A fuel, such as coal, oil, or natural gas, formed in the earth from plant or animal remains.

machine A combination of parts that transmit forces, motion, and energy to perform a task.

neutron An uncharged atomic particle that is present in all known atomic nuclei except the hydrogen nucleus.

nucleus The central part of an atom.

philosopher A person who seeks wisdom.

power Another word for energy, which means the ability to do work.

power plant A building in which electric power is generated.

proton A tiny particle that occurs in the nucleus of every atom and has a positive electric charge.

solar power The energy from sunlight that is used to run machinery.

turbine An engine with a central driving shaft that spins around. The shaft has winglike parts that are whirled around by the pressure of water, steam, or gas.

waterpower The energy from moving water that is used to run machinery.

windmill A mill or a machine worked by the wind turning sails or vanes at the top of a tower.

FOR MORE INFORMATION

Books

Berne, Emma Carlson. *Shocking! Electricity* (Energy Everywhere). New York, NY: Rosen Publishing, Inc., 2013.

Kramer, Barbara. *National Geographic Readers: Thomas Edison* (Readers Bios). Washington, DC: National Geographic Children's Books, 2014.

Monroe, Tilda. *What Do You Know About Electricity?* (20 Questions: Physical Science). New York, NY: Rosen Publishing, Inc., 2011.

Royston, Angela. *Electricity* (Science Corner). New York, NY: Rosen Publishing, Inc., 2012.

Van Fleet, Carmella. *Explore Electricity! With 25 Great Projects* (Explore Your World). White River Junction, VT: Nomad Press, 2013.

Websites

Because of the changing nature of internet links, Rosen Publishing has developed an online list of websites related to the subject of this book. This site is updated regularly. Please use this link to access the list:

http://www.rosenlinks.com/LFO/electrical

INDEX